Kylie Minogue

Princess of Pop

This paperback edition published in 2016
First published in hardback in 2015

Copyright © Wayland, 2015

Editor: Elizabeth Brent

Produced for Wayland by Calcium
All rights reserved.
Dewey Number: 782.4'2166'092-dc23
ISBN: 978 0 7502 9048 7
Library e-book ISBN: 978 0 7502 9047 0
10 9 8 7 6 5 4 3 2 1

MIX
Paper from
responsible sources
FSC® C104740

Wayland
An imprint of
Hachette Children's Group
Part of Hodder & Stoughton
Carmelite House
50 Victoria Embankment
London EC4Y 0DZ

An Hachette UK Company
www.hachette.co.uk

www.hachettechildrens.co.uk

Picture acknowledgements:

Key: b=bottom, t=top, r=right, l=left,
m=middle, bgd=background

Cover: Dreamstime: Featureflash;
Shutterstock: Featureflash (inset).
Alamy: InterFoto 8, Trinity Mirror/
Mirrorpix 6; Corbis: Steffan Rousseau/
Pool/Reuters 27; Dreamstime: Albo
30b, Featureflash 30t, S Bukley 29; Getty Images: Mark
Cuthbert/UK Press 23, Express/Stringer 13, Dave Hogan/Hulton
Archive 9, 10, 11, 12, Mick Hutson/Redferns 16, Eamonn McCormack/
WireImage 24, Robert Pearce/The Sydney Morning Herald/Fairfax
Media 21, Bertrand Rindoff Petroff 17, Tim Roney 14–15; Rex
Features: Julie Kiriacoudis/Newspix 7; Shutterstock: Albo 22, Andrey
Bayda 5b, Christian Bertrand 20l, Simon Burchell/Featureflash 18,
Helga Esteb 5t, Featureflash 4, Henry Harris/Featureflash 20r, Jaguar
PS 25, Andrea Raffin 19, S Bukley 1, Paul Smith/Featureflash 2.

Kylie Minogue

Contents

KYLIE MINOGUE:
Princess of Pop

Kylie Minogue started her career as a young actress in an Australian television series called *Neighbours*. Today, she is so famous that she's often known simply by her first name. Kylie is a singer, actress, dancer and television presenter. The talented performer has dominated the charts for more than 25 years.

NAME: Kylie Ann Minogue

BORN: 28 May 1968

BIRTHPLACE: Melbourne, Australia

SCHOOL: Camberwell High School, Melbourne, Australia

OCCUPATION: Actress, singer and dancer

FAMOUS FOR: Starring in Neighbours, selling more than 70 million records

LIKES: Playing scrabble, reading, walking, gardening

Melbourne, Australia

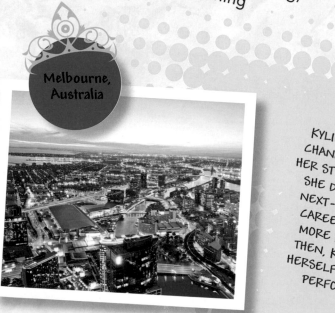

Did You Know?

KYLIE HAS NEVER BEEN AFRAID TO CHANGE HER IMAGE, AND HAS KEPT HER STYLE COOL AND CONTEMPORARY. SHE DROPPED THE BUBBLY, GIRL-NEXT-DOOR IMAGE OF HER EARLY CAREER TO SHOW A WILDER AND MORE REBELLIOUS SIDE. SINCE THEN, KYLIE HAS TRANSFORMED HERSELF INTO A SHOW-STOPPING PERFORMER AND DANCER.

Young Ambition

Kylie in her role as Charlene in *Neighbours* in 1988.

Kylie was born and brought up in the city of Melbourne, Australia. She has a younger sister and brother, Dannii and Brendan. Kylie's dad, Ron, was an accountant and her mum, Carol, was a dancer whose family had moved to Australia from Wales.

none of the Minogue children were pushed into the performing arts, although Carol encouraged both her daughters to learn musical instruments. Kylie studied the piano, flute and violin until she was 13 years old.

Kylie's sister Dannii is also in the media spotlight, as a singer and television presenter. Kylie's brother Brendan works as a film cameraman.

SPEAKING ABOUT HER CHILDHOOD LOVE OF ENTERTAINING, KYLIE HAS SAID:

'WHEN I WAS EIGHT, MY PALS AND I WENT UP TO MY BEDROOM, PUT ON OUR PARTY FROCKS AND MIMED TO ABBA RECORDS USING BROOM HANDLES AS MICROPHONES.'

Kylie's younger sister, Dannii, was spotted by a talent scout in a supermarket when out with her mother. She was invited to audition for a role in the television show *The Sullivans*. Carol didn't want Kylie to be left out so she took her along, too. In the end, it was Kylie, and not Dannii, who was offered a part.

Kylie's role in *The Sullivans* didn't last long, however, because her character was killed off. Later, Dannii took on her older sister's part, appearing as a 'vision'! For a while, it was Dannii who shone as the child star and, as they progressed, the sisters both built up singing careers. However, it was Kylie who was to become a superstar.

Like her sister Kylie, Dannii is often in the media spotlight.

Pop Princess

The media has always delighted in comparing the ups and downs of the Minogue sisters. Both Kylie and Dannii achieved success in their own way and are supportive of each other. When Dannii was a judge on the British television show *The X Factor*, she asked her sister Kylie to come and help her. When Kylie returned to performing after her cancer treatment, Dannii went on tour with her.

The Girl Next Door

In 1985, Kylie was given a role in the television show *The Hendersons*. The show was popular and revealed Kylie's talent. However, her real break came in 1986 when she was given the part of Charlene in *Neighbours*.

Neighbours is a hugely popular soap opera, broadcast in both Australia and the United Kingdom. In the show, Kylie took on the role of Charlene, a teenage tomboy who worked as a mechanic.

Kylie acted alongside real-life friend Jason Donovan, who played the part of Scott. In Neighbours, Charlene and Scott were girlfriend and boyfriend. There was much speculation that Kylie and Jason were also a couple in real life. Kylie and Jason were dating, but they kept their relationship secret for quite some time.

'I WORK A 12-HOUR DAY ON NEIGHBOURS STARTING AT 6.30 AM EVERY MORNING. I'M IN THE STUDIO UNTIL 7.15 PM.'

Pop Princess

In 2014, Kylie was offered the chance to appear once more in *Neighbours* to mark its 30th anniversary. However, she decided not to return to the show that had made her a household name.

In 1987, the on-screen marriage of Charlene and Scott attracted a record number of viewers to the programme in Australia. When the episode was broadcast in the United Kingdom, it was the third-most watched programme in the country that year.

The Australian postal service even issued a stamp that featured the couple in their wedding clothes!

'YOU HAVE TO BE LUCKY TO GO STRAIGHT FROM SCHOOL INTO A JOB WHICH MAKES YOU FAMOUS THROUGHOUT THE WORLD.'

Singing Solo

Kylie didn't set out to be a singer, although she once sang on *Young Talent Time*, a television talent show that featured her sister, Dannii. Kylie's career as a recording artist took off after she sang in a benefit concert with other *Neighbours* actors. A producer heard her sing, and a record label called Mushroom Records offered the young Kylie a recording contract soon after.

In 1987, Kylie recorded her debut single *The Locomotion* for Mushroom Records. It was a great hit – for seven weeks it was Number One in the Australian singles chart. Kylie's career as a pop star was taking off.

Fired up by the success of *The Locomotion*, Kylie travelled to London to meet with a well-established music writing and production team, called Stock, Aitken and Waterman.

Kylie had flown halfway round the world to meet them, but the team had forgotten she was coming! They asked Kylie to wait outside the studios while the producers quickly wrote some lyrics. They gave them to Kylie, and within an hour she had recorded a song.

The song was *I Should Be So Lucky*. It went on to become a huge hit and propelled Kylie firmly towards stardom.

Pop Princess

Stock, Aitken and Waterman were surprised by the success of *I Should Be So Lucky*. People loved the catchy tune and lyrics, and Kylie's cute and bubbly persona – a pop star was born. This was the start of her partnership with Stock, Aitken and Waterman. At around this time, too, Terry Blamey became Kylie's manager, a role he would hold for more than 25 years.

AT AN AWARDS CEREMONY IN 2012, KYLIE SAID: 'TERRY, THANK YOU SO MUCH FOR EVERYTHING. FOR HELPING A 19-YEAR-OLD GIRL TAKE ON THE WORLD AND BECOME A WOMAN AND AN ARTIST.'

Kylie with gold discs for the singles *I Should Be So Lucky* and *Got to Be Certain* in 1988.

Hard Work

Kylie was working long hours filming *Neighbours* and concentrating on her singing career. She didn't have much time for friends or fun, but she knew that the effort spent on her career would be worth it.

In 1988, Kylie won an incredible four Logie Awards (Australian television awards), including the Gold Logie for the Most Popular TV Personality, which was voted for by the public. *Neighbours* co-star Jason Donovan also won an award for Most Popular Actor. The cast and crew went out to celebrate the show and the stars' success, but Kylie instead went back to her hotel room by herself. At just 20 years old, she was feeling the pressure of her exhausting work schedule and was overwhelmed by her growing fame.

After two years of playing Charlene, Kylie made the decision to leave *Neighbours*. She decided it was time to move on from the series that had thrown her into the spotlight, and to develop her work elsewhere.

Kylie and Jason attend the London premiere of the film *Batman* in 1989.

Both Jason and Kylie were working hard to develop their singing careers. Eventually, after much speculation in the press, the couple confessed to their real-life romance. In 1989, they recorded the song *Especially for You* together. It was released in time for Christmas, and was a smash hit.

Pop Princess

In Kylie's early career, her singing was often criticised. Some people said she was only successful because of her popularity as Charlene in *Neighbours*. Certain radio stations even refused to play her music! It took a while before the music industry began to respect Kylie's talent as an artist.

In the 1980s, Kylie's busy work schedule meant that she was travelling all over the world.

DANNII OFTEN SPOKE UP FOR HER OLDER SISTER AGAINST CRITICISM OF HER MUSIC: 'IT'S TERRIBLE FOR KYLIE...THEY CLAIM HER RECORDS ARE NAFF. YET EVERY TIME THERE IS A POP POLL, KYLIE COMES OUT ON TOP.'

Moving On

Having left *Neighbours*, the young actress also left Australia and moved to London, where she still lives today. She also began to shed the girl-next-door image that her fans were used to.

In a brave move, Kylie took on a gritty role playing a 15-year-old girl battling drink and drug problems in the film *The Delinquents*. Critics didn't like the film and were negative about Kylie's acting, but Kylie herself remained positive and confident about her decision.

> KYLIE ON HER ROLE
> IN *THE DELINQUENTS*:
> '...I STILL FEEL I HAVE DONE THE RIGHT THING...AT LEAST I FEEL LIKE I HAVE GROWN UP. I DON'T THINK I'LL LOSE ANY FANS. I MAY GAIN WIDER ACCEPTANCE.'

Kylie was a rising star in the music world. However, some people felt she had been disloyal to the people and programme that started her career. Kylie had made some comments about *Neighbours* that upset and annoyed her fellow actors. They felt she should have more respect for the Australian soap.

Work commitments meant that Kylie and Jason spent a lot of time apart, often on opposite sides of the world. Their relationship as boyfriend and girlfriend broke down, but they remained good friends. And for Kylie, there was a new and hugely influential man in her life – Michael Hutchence. Kylie had met Hutchence briefly in 1987, but it was a few years before they became a couple.

Kylie appearing on UK television show *Going Live!* in 1989.

Michael Hutchence fronted the rock band INXS. At six feet tall and with a reputation for wild parties, Hutchence seemed an unlikely partner for Kylie. However, much to the surprise of their friends and the people around them, Kylie and Michael fell deeply in love.

Pop Princess

From early speculation about her relationship with Jason, to surprise at her relationship with Hutchence, Kylie's love life is often in the news. She had a long relationship with the French actor Olivier Martinez, with whom she lived in Paris. There, Kylie learnt to speak French fluently.

15

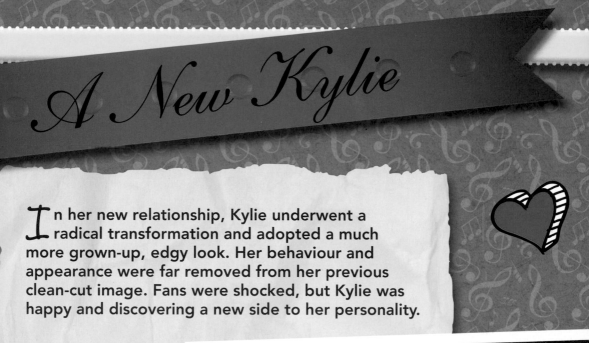

In her new relationship, Kylie underwent a radical transformation and adopted a much more grown-up, edgy look. Her behaviour and appearance were far removed from her previous clean-cut image. Fans were shocked, but Kylie was happy and discovering a new side to her personality.

During this time, Kylie's music was changing, too. She left behind her trademark pop music and ventured into club and dance music, which was directed at an older audience. In 1992, Kylie left Stock, Aitken and Waterman and signed up with a new record label called Deconstruction.

For two years, Kylie and Hutchence were happy together but their relationship broke down in 1991. Despite this, they remained good friends. After the split from Michael, Kylie threw herself into her work.

Years later, in 1997, Kylie was shocked to learn that Michael had been found dead, at the age of just 37. The exact circumstances of his death have never been clear, and Kylie was devastated.

ON HER RELATIONSHIP WITH HUTCHENCE: 'IT WAS GREAT LOVE, AND IT WAS TRUE HEARTBREAK.'

Top of the Pops

K ylie has been a major presence in the world of music and performance for more than 25 years, and she is still producing record-breaking singles and show-stopping tours today.

Pop Princess

Kylie's much-anticipated album *Impossible Princess* was due for release in 1997. However, it was renamed *Kylie Minogue* after the sudden death of Princess Diana just two weeks before the album's release date.

These are just some of Kylie's top hits:

1987 **The Locomotion**

1987 **I Should Be So Lucky** (from *Kylie*, her debut album)

1988 **Especially for You** (with Jason Donovan)

1989 **Hand on Your Heart** (*Enjoy Yourself* album)

1990 **Better the Devil You Know** (*Rhythm of Love* album)

1991 **Give Me Just a Little More Time** (*Let's Get to It* album)

1995 **Where the Wild Roses Grow** (a duet with Nick Cave and the Bad Seeds from Nick Cave's *Murder Ballads* album)

1997 **Did It Again** (*Impossible Princess/Kylie Minogue* album)

2000 **Spinning Around** (*Light Years* album)

2000 **Kids** (a duet with Robbie Williams from the *Light Years* album)

2002 **Can't Get You Out of My Head** (*Fever* album)

2002 **Come Into My World** (*Fever* album)

2003 **Slow** (*Body Language* album)

2004 **I Believe in You** (*Ultimate Kylie* album)

2007 **Wow** (*X* album)

2010 **All the Lovers** (*Aphrodite* album)

2012 **Timebomb** (*non-album* single)

2014 **Into the Blue** (*Kiss Me Once* album)

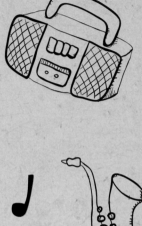

On leaving *Neighbours* and meeting Hutchence, Kylie began to move away from the manufactured image of a pop star. She worked with other artists who also influenced her developing style.

Kylie's artistic partnerships included working with the indie artist Nick Cave and the rock band Manic Street Preachers.

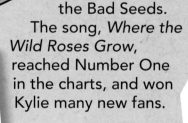

'FOR SO LONG I HAD SUCH AN EMBARRASSMENT ABOUT THE EARLY DAYS...I WAS RUNNING AS FAST AS I COULD AWAY FROM IT, BUT NOW I REALISE IT WAS ACTUALLY PRETTY COOL.'

In 1995, Kylie recorded a duet with Nick Cave and his band, the Bad Seeds. The song, *Where the Wild Roses Grow*, reached Number One in the charts, and won Kylie many new fans.

Nick Cave

Manic Street Preachers

The following year, Kylie made a surprise appearance without fanfare, make-up or glitzy clothes at the Poetry Olympics at the Royal Albert Hall, London. There, persuaded by Nick Cave, she recited the lyrics to her hit song from 1987, *I Should Be So Lucky*. The crowd loved it, despite Kylie's worries about how it would be perceived. By reciting the 'poem', Kylie was acknowledging her past image and showing that she did not take herself too seriously.

Kylie at the funeral of Michael Hutchence.

AT THE START OF THE POETRY OLYMPICS, KYLIE SAID: 'HI. I DIDN'T EXPECT TO BE HERE TODAY BUT I AM AND I AM GOING TO RECITE SOMETHING I DIDN'T WRITE. "IN MY IMAGINATION, THERE IS NO COMPLICATION, I DREAM ABOUT YOU ALL THE TIME..."'

Despite her experimentations with her artistic style, 1997 was a difficult year for Kylie. She was rocked by the death of her former boyfriend, Michael Hutchence. She had released singles, but was taking a long time to record an album. When *Impossible Princess (Kylie Minogue)* was released after three years in the making, it was not a great success with critics or fans. Kylie was struggling to find her own style and was dropped by Deconstruction Records.

The Show Can't Go On

Determined to reignite her career, Kylie joined a new record label called Parlophone. Then, in 2000, she bounced back onto the music scene with a dance-pop album called *Light Years*.

Kylie seemed to have found her natural style and confidence, and was becoming well-respected in the music industry. After 2000, Kylie's music, videos and tours became stunning displays of dancing, music and performance. Her shows featured extravagant, spectacular routines and flamboyant costumes, and there were often about seven costume changes in each show! Fashion designers were desperate to design outfits for Kylie, both on and off stage.

ON SEEING THE DRESS THAT KYLIE HAD PERSONALISED, JULIEN MACDONALD SAID: 'THAT NIGHT MY HEART STOPPED. KYLIE HAD CUT THE DRESS. SHE DID LOOK FANTASTIC THOUGH, AND IT MADE ALL THE FRONT PAGES, SO ALL WAS FORGIVEN.'

Pop Princess

Designer Julien Macdonald was shocked to see one of his dresses worn by Kylie when she was performing at the Brit Awards in 2003. Kylie had cut the dress to the top of the thigh!

As well as working on her singing career, Kylie occasionally returned to her acting roots. In 2001, she took on the role of the Green Fairy in the film *Moulin Rouge*, alongside Ewan McGregor and Nicole Kidman.

Kylie smiles for the cameras at the premiere of *Moulin Rouge*.

However, in 2005, Kylie's world was rocked when she was diagnosed with breast cancer. She was in the middle of a major tour (*Showgirl: The Greatest Hits Tour*) and had been due to perform at Glastonbury Festival, but her diagnosis forced her to cancel both. After Kylie announced that she had cancer, there was a dramatic rise in the number of women who attended screenings to check for signs of breast cancer.

'I WAS SO LOOKING FORWARD TO BRINGING THE SHOWGIRL TOUR TO AUSTRALIA AND TO GLASTONBURY AND AM SORRY TO HAVE TO DISAPPOINT MY FANS. NEVERTHELESS, HOPEFULLY ALL WILL WORK OUT FINE AND I'LL BE BACK WITH YOU ALL AGAIN SOON.'

Kylie's Return

Kylie took time out for her cancer treatment and her recovery, although during this time she managed to write a children's book, called *The Showgirl Princess!* After a full recovery, Kylie returned to performing.

In 2014, Kylie took over from Jessie J as a judge on the hit television show *The Voice*.

KYLIE, SPEAKING ABOUT HER RECOVERY FROM CANCER:

'A DAY DOES NOT GO BY WITHOUT ME THINKING ABOUT IT. THERE ARE DAYS WHEN I FEEL AN INCREDIBLE ANGER, OTHERS WHEN I SAY THAT I WAS VERY LUCKY IN MY MISFORTUNE.'

Kylie is never content to sit back and take things easy, and continuously explores new avenues of work. Recently, she spent a year as a coach and mentor on both the UK and Australian versions of *The Voice*, a singing television talent show in which she coached aspiring singers.

Like many other stars, Kylie has also branched out into selling products under her name. She has produced eight perfumes and has her own brand of homeware, including products such as candles and cushions.

Kylie has always supported many charities. She was the National Society for the Prevention of Cruelty to Children's (NSPCC) first celebrity ambassador, and has helped to raise awareness for its cause. Following her illness, Kylie has become particularly involved in raising money and awareness for breast cancer charities. In 2011, Kylie was recognised for her contribution to breast cancer awareness when she was awarded an honorary Doctorate of Health Sciences (D.H.Sc.) degree by Anglia Ruskin University in the United Kingdom.

Kylie dazzles at the premiere of the film Hercules.

Pop Princess

Kylie appeared in the television series *Dr Who* as a waitress on board a spaceship! She also made a documentary called *White Diamond*, which was a behind-the-scenes look at her resumed *Showgirl* tour.

Kylie has long been one of the most photographed women in the world. In recent years, she has taken more control over her image and styling. She has often been supported by long-term friend and stylist William Baker, who also directed *White Diamond*. Kylie met Baker in 1994 when she went into a clothes shop in London where he worked as a sales assistant. He gave Kylie a lot of suggestions about styling, and the two became working partners and firm friends.

Kylie has received numerous awards and honours. Here are just a few of them:

1987 Silver Logie Award for Most Popular Actress.

1988 Gold Logie Award for Most Popular Personality on Australian Television.

1989 The first waxwork model of Kylie at Madame Tussauds in London (since then, there have been another three wax models of Kylie).

1990 Logie Award for Most Popular Music Video (*Never Too Late*).

1998 An Achievement Award from the Australian government for her contribution to Australian exports.

2000 Kylie performed at the closing ceremony of the Sydney Olympics.

2002 Won two Brit Awards – Best International Female Artist and Best International Album for *Fever*.

Pop Princess

The wedding dress worn by Kylie as Charlene in *Neighbours* is on display in Melbourne Museum. A picture of Kylie, signed in pink lipstick, is displayed in Australia's National Portrait Gallery.

> KYLIE BEGAN HER CAREER AS AN ACTRESS. SHE THEN FOUND HUGE FAME AS A SINGER, BUT SHE SAYS: 'PEOPLE SEE ME AS KYLIE THE SINGER. IT WOULD BE A DREAM FOR ME TO BE TAKEN SERIOUSLY AS AN ACTRESS.'

2004 Won a Grammy Award for Best Dance Recording for the single *Come Into My World.*

2008 Made an Officer of the Order of the British Empire (OBE) for services to music.

2008 Appointed a Chevalier (knight) of the Ordre des Arts et des Lettres by the French government. This is the junior grade of France's highest cultural honour. Kylie was given the award for her contribution to the enrichment of French culture.

2011 Entered the Australian Recording Industry Association Hall of Fame.

2012 Appointed Creative Ambassador for Sydney (Australia) New Year's Eve Celebrations.

2014 Performed at the end of the Commonwealth Games in Glasgow, Scotland.

Kylie poses with her OBE at Buckingham Palace, London, in 2008.

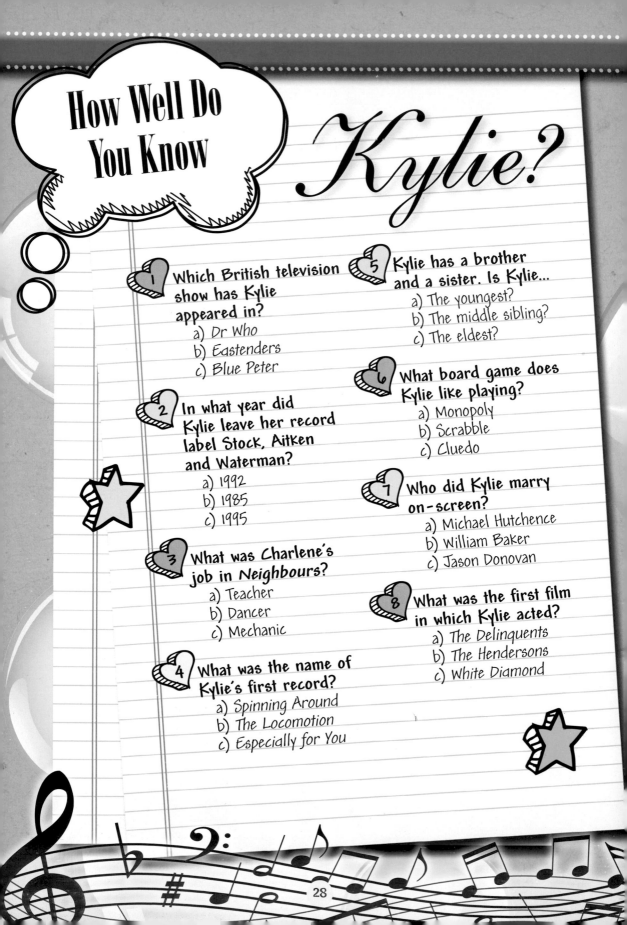

How Well Do You Know Kylie?

1 Which British television show has Kylie appeared in?
a) Dr Who
b) Eastenders
c) Blue Peter

2 In what year did Kylie leave her record label Stock, Aitken and Waterman?
a) 1992
b) 1985
c) 1995

3 What was Charlene's job in *Neighbours*?
a) Teacher
b) Dancer
c) Mechanic

4 What was the name of Kylie's first record?
a) Spinning Around
b) The Locomotion
c) Especially for You

5 Kylie has a brother and a sister. Is Kylie...
a) The youngest?
b) The middle sibling?
c) The eldest?

6 What board game does Kylie like playing?
a) Monopoly
b) Scrabble
c) Cluedo

7 Who did Kylie marry on-screen?
a) Michael Hutchence
b) William Baker
c) Jason Donovan

8 What was the first film in which Kylie acted?
a) The Delinquents
b) The Hendersons
c) White Diamond

9 At which event was Kylie Creative Ambassador?
a) The 2012 UK Olympics
b) The Sydney 2012 New Year's Eve Celebrations
c) The 2014 Commonwealth Games

10 When was Kylie born?
a) 1968
b) 1965
c) 1970

Answers

1. a) Dr Who
2. a) 1992
3. c) Mechanic
4. b) *The Locomotion*
5. c) The eldest
6. b) Scrabble
7. c) Jason Donovan
8. a) *The Delinquents*
9. b) The Sydney 2012 New Year's Eve Celebrations
10. a) 1968

Discover more about Kylie's work and interests on her website:

www.kylie.com

Quote sources

Page 6 http://m.imdb.com; **Page 8** Kylie, Story of a Survivor by Virginia Blackburn, 2007; **Page 9** Kylie, Story of a Survivor by Virginia Blackburn, 2007; **Page 11** www.music.week.com; **Page 12** Kylie, Story of a Survivor by Virginia Blackburn, 2007; **Page 13** Kylie, Story of a Survivor by Virginia Blackburn, 2007; **Page 14** Kylie, Story of a Survivor by Virginia Blackburn, 2007; **Page 17** Australia's 60 Minutes; **Page 20** Kylie, Story of a Survivor by Virginia Blackburn, 2007; **Page 22** BBC News, 2007; **Page 23** The Guardian; **Page 24** www.huffingtonpost.co.uk, 2014; **Page 26** http://m.imdb.com

Glossary

accountant a person who looks after the financial accounts of a person or an organisation

broadcast to transmit on television or radio

cancer a disease that can affect different parts of the body

contemporary modern

debut first

diagnosis the identification of a disease

documentary a factual story that is filmed

dominated kept a strong presence

extravagant over the top, lavish

flamboyant showy

fluently able to speak a language well

honorary given in recognition of someone's achievements, without them fulfilling the usual requirements

indie independent

influential has an influence

lyrics the words of a song

media the press, including newspapers, radio and television

mentor advisor

perceived thought of

Poetry Olympics an event featuring many different poets and types of poem

producer a person responsible for managing the recording of music

propelled pushed forwards

recording contract when a record label agrees to sell and promote the work of a singer or band

reignite revive, bring back

soap opera a long-running television drama

speculation rumour or gossip

stylist someone who helps create an image or an outfit for someone or something

transformation a noticeable or dramatic change

Index